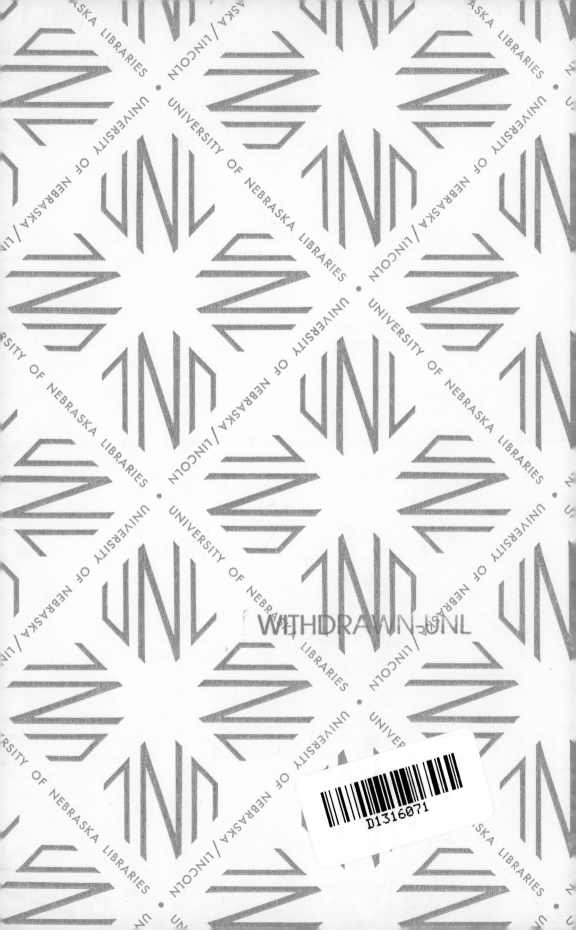

TORONTO

John de Visser

TORONTO

John de Visser

Introduction and Notes by
WILLIAM TOYE

Toronto
OXFORD UNIVERSITY PRESS
1975

© Oxford University Press Canada 1975. ISBN 19–540243–X. Printed in Canada by the Bryant Press Limited 1234–8765

INTRODUCTION

The Toronto area first attracted the attention of white men in the French régime. A small trading post was maintained for ten years after 1720 near the mouth of the Humber River, which provided a route that led by portages, lakes, and rivers to the Northwest. Another small fort was built there in 1750, and in 1750-1 a second larger one was constructed a little to the east, at the foot of present-day Dufferin Street. It was called Fort Rouillé, after the Ministre de la Marine, but was commonly known as Fort Toronto. (This Indian name was ascribed to various places in the second half of the seventeenth century: Lake Simcoe, Georgian Bay, the country between, the Severn River. In the eighteenth century it appeared on maps south of Lake Simcoe, referring in particular to the Humber River.) After Niagara fell to British forces in 1759, Fort Toronto was burned by its French occupants, who retreated to Montreal.

In 1787, under the Governor-in-Chief of British North America, Lord Dorchester, some quarter of a million acres north of Lake Ontario were purchased from the Indians for £1,700 (and cloth and axes). A year later he had the territory surveyed, but a town on the present site of Toronto did not become a reality until 1793, under the new Lieutenant-Governor of Upper Canada, John Graves Simcoe, who was impressed by the excellent harbour. With a sandbar near the mouth of the Don River joining the mainland to a group of islands that sheltered the bay, it was 'the best Harbour on the Lakes', according to Simcoe, who envisaged a naval arsenal there. He arrived from Niagara with his family in July to begin settlement. The Simcoes spent the following winter in a 'Canvas House' (at the foot of today's Bathurst Street), while the Queen's Rangers proceeded with the felling of trees and the building of log dwellings.

A town was laid out on a grid system—ten blocks near the mouth of the Don River, bounded by George, Duke (now Adelaide), Berkeley, and Front Streets. (All the later main streets of Toronto were based on this grid, in defiance of the valleys and hills that characterized its topography.) In August it was given the name of York, after Frederick, Duke of York, the second son of George III who had recently been victorious in battle. Later in the year it was designated the temporary capital of Upper Canada, a position that gave it many advantages, not the least of which was that it became the home of some educated and able men. In time it was accepted as the permanent capital.

Simcoe left in 1796 and under his successor, the Administrator Peter Russell, the town was extended westward to Peter Street and north to Lot (Queen) Street—beyond which was the forest. But for the next twenty years York remained little more than a village, and an unprepossessing one at that, set in a swamp, with muddy streets lined with plain wooden buildings—though the houses of government officials, on spacious lots, had some pretensions and were well designed. In 1797 the population was 241. It increased very slowly: ten years later it was only

414, and in 1812, the year the United States declared war on Britain, it was 703. Residents were English, Irish, Scots, and American. The senior government officials, with a few wealthy landowners and merchants, formed an upper class; the lower classes were composed of clerks, tradesmen, and labourers. Before 1812 there were hotels and boarding houses, taverns, lawyers' offices, a wagon factory, a tinsmith shop, a printing office, and six or seven stores, including a bookshop and library. The storekeepers were important in the life of the town and several of them became prosperous. One of them, Quetton St George, built a home-cum-shop at King and Frederick Streets that was an imposing two-storey brick building roofed with tin (1807)—the first brick house in York. King Street was the main east-west thoroughfare, extending from the Don River in the east to Peter Street. It contained most of the shops and, to the east, a boarding house, Jordan's Hotel, and Maryville Lodge (1797), the large house and grounds of D.W. Smith, the Surveyor-General. The 'English Church', a small unpainted wooden building owned by the Church of England, stood at the corner of King and Church in a grove of trees. Erected in 1807, it was the only church until 1818. (It was not officially named St James' until 1828.) The Parliament Buildings were to the east of town and the Garrison (at the foot of Bathurst Street) was two miles to the west. By 1799 there were two long-distance roads leading out of York. Dundas Street, begun in 1793, was opened to the Grand River in the west; and Yonge Street, begun in 1794 at Eglinton Avenue, was opened north to Lake Simcoe. In 1799 Asa Danforth was contracted to build a road eastward to the Bay of Quinte.

York was jolted out of its sense of being a sleepy, isolated backwater when the War of 1812 was declared and it realized that it might be subjected to an American attack. On April 26, 1813 an American squadron of fourteen sail was seen off Scarborough Bluffs and the next day there was a landing below the Garrison. In the engagement that followed, the small, ineptly led force under General Shaeffe was totally defeated. After blowing up the powder magazine—and killing or wounding over a hundred men on each side—Shaeffe decided to retreat to Kingston and York capitulated. During the four days the Americans stayed in town there was some looting (possibly by both Americans and Canadians), and the Parliament Buildings and other properties, including the Government House (1800), were destroyed.

From 1815, when the War of 1812 ended, to 1834, the year York was incorporated as the city of Toronto, the town underwent its first major phase of development. In 1815 there were about 700 people. In 1834 the population was 9,254. The merchants, who had done well from the war, had to weather a depression, but everything changed with the development of wholesale trade, when the first great period of immigration into what is now southwestern Ontario began in the late 1820s and the hinterland opened up. Some large new public buildings improved the previous village-like appearance of York—though a sophisticated Englishwoman, Anna Jameson, who visited it in 1836, called it 'ill-built' and 'most strangely mean and melancholy' in winter. There was Osgoode Hall (1829) on Queen Street (the core of the present east wing), the home of the Law Society of

Upper Canada. There were the new Parliament Buildings on Front Street at Simcoe (1832), the governor's residence in the block behind (1828), and Upper Canada College (1830) in the block behind that on King Street. (Here was the intersection later called 'Education, Legislation, Salvation, and Damnation', occupied by the College, the governor's residence, St Andrew's Presbyterian Church (1876), and a tavern.) To the west of the College was the York General Hospital (1829). To the east, at Church Street, a large new stone building for St James' replaced the renovated blue-and-white wooden one in 1833. King Street also boasted a Court House and jail on the north side immediately west of St James'; its shops, several of them now made of brick, formed a sedate row of Georgian buildings. In 1831 a new market building that later housed the municipal offices was erected at Jarvis Street.

Some of the members of the upper class lived in impressive houses on Front Street facing the bay, on Duke Street, and on large estates to the northwest, beyond the town's limits. Two imposing Neo-Classical houses of this period can still be seen: the red brick house (1822) of Chief Justice Sir William Campbell, which was originally on Duke Street (it has been moved to University and Queen), and The Grange (1817), the house of D'Arcy Boulton Jr.

In 1834 there were nine churches or chapels in Toronto. The immigrants were not only Anglican, but Roman Catholic or various kinds of Nonconformists, and each denomination had to have its own church. Many of these people were experienced tradesmen who greatly improved the available services. Ulstermen and Irish Catholics, Highland and Lowland Scots, and Yorkshiremen et al., they produced a middle class, which had not existed significantly before, and put a British stamp on the town. (Some of these immigrants who were both poor and incapable of working created a slum.) The new arrivals also introduced controversy into the political life of York.

The government of Upper Canada fostered the development of a local oligarchy. It was made up of a group of educated, privileged men with British ties and sympathies who were conservative in politics and firm believers in the interdependence of Church and State. Many of them were appointed members of the upper house or Legislative Council and the 'cabinet' or Executive Council—neither of which was answerable, or responsible, to the lower house or Assembly—and these men more or less ran the province.

The serene tenor of their enlightened despotism was broken in the early twenties by the arrival, with the immigrants, of democratic ideals. People now offered various degrees of opposition to government for reasons of class, religious persuasion, or personal grievance. The political activities of York were thereafter inflamed by the disagreements of noisy and often bitter factions. Most of the reformers were moderate, but a radical group was brought into being by an impetuous, rabble-rousing Scot, William Lyon Mackenzie. His newspaper, the *Colonial Advocate*—one of ten journals published in York at the time—publicized the grievances of town labourers and poverty-stricken farmers, among whom Mackenzie became a popular hero. (He was elected numerous times to the

Assembly and was the first mayor of Toronto—for nine months.) As his political views became more and more extreme and his behaviour irrational, a flare-up was inevitable. Some of his rural supporters were intrigued by his talk of rebellion, wild though it was, and followed him in an uprising that took the form of two skirmishes. One, on December 5, 1837, was east of Yonge, below Maitland; the other, on the 7th, was two miles north, near Yonge and Davisville, south of the rebels' headquarters at Montgomery's Tavern (at Montgomery Avenue and Yonge). In both cases the insurgents were put to flight. These events in the Rebellion of 1837, and other disturbances in Lower Canada, led to an investigation, to the union of Upper and Lower Canada in 1841, and to the introduction of responsible government in 1848. They also produced an aversion to radicalism in Toronto and the strong Conservative tendencies that remain in the city, and the province, to this day. 'The wild and rabid toryism of Toronto,' Charles Dickens wrote in 1842, 'is, I speak seriously, appalling.'

During the rest of the nineteenth century, and in spite of two depressions, Toronto followed a course of steady development in trade, finance, and manufacturing, helped greatly by immigration, by a rich agricultural hinterland, and by a harbour that took on more and more importance as canals were constructed in the east and west. In 1851 the population was 30,775 and the city's northern boundary was Bloor Street, beyond which was the Village of Yorkville. In 1891, when the northern outskirts were approaching St Clair in the north, the population was 181,200—strongly British in composition, mainly Protestant, and Tory. A fever of construction activity raised the pretensions of Torontonians considerably. The downtown gave rise to public buildings, churches, banks, educational institutions, two opera houses, several theatres, and houses for the wealthy, in all of which Victorian architects drew upon multifarious architectural details from the past to represent the pride and prosperity of the present.

Toronto's importance as a business centre made it the hub of a network of railways, to which the waterfront fell prey. Extensive landfill put a distance between Front Street and the harbour, and by the 1890s the waterfront was a jumble of utilitarian buildings through which railway tracks cut a desolate swath (a use of the area that is only with difficulty being revised today, when the loss to the city is at last being keenly felt). Economic expansion was also aided by the vigour and enterprise of Scots, Irish, and English businessmen, many of them Presbyterians and Methodists in whom the work ethic, keen business instincts, and the accumulation of wealth were combined with a deep and narrow piety. These two strains, business and religion, made an imprint on the city that was both physical and psychological. The tall-spired Gothic Revival churches and the later heavily proportioned Romanesque-style tabernacles that appeared in great profusion during the nineteenth century were endowed by the same men who controlled the banks, investment firms, insurance companies and owned the factories and general stores that gave a soberly affluent commercial look to the main streets of 'Toronto the Good'. Financiers and wealthy merchants were of one mind with many less prosperous people in believing that Sunday should be strictly preserved as a day of rest and church-going, and that intemperance (in a city of some three hundred taverns) was a fundamental social problem. Advocates of temperance preached vigorously, using cautionary tales that easily came to hand—for 'Drunkenness is very common in Toronto', wrote one writer in an exposé of the underside of city life entitled *Of Toronto the Good* (1898). This was the period that gave birth to those civic characteristics that outsiders deplored or made fun of for many decades: a boring puritanism and smugness, a colonial blandness that the ultra-loyal Anglo-Saxon majority imposed on their institutions and social life, and anti-Catholic bigotry, of which members of the Irish-Protestant Orange Order provided many examples.

Between 1906 and 1912 the villages of North Rosedale, Deer Park, East Toronto, West Toronto, Midway (east of the Don), Dovercourt and Earlscourt, North Toronto, and Moore Park were annexed to Toronto. These far-flung areas—which even now, when they are city neighbourhoods, have a character and a community spirit of their own—were joined to the centre and to each other by a transportation system that has always been considered an important element in the proper functioning of the city. It began with horse-drawn omnibuses; progressed to open electric-powered streetcars; to the Peter Witt cars that were used from 1921 until the fifties and were introduced by the newly formed Toronto Transportation Commission; to buses and the sleek, efficient streetcars that first saw service in 1938 (389 cars in this design are still being used); and to the opening of the Yonge Street subway line in 1954, which brought an end to ninety-three years of streetcar service on Toronto's main street.

While Victorian and Edwardian mansions along Sherbourne, Jarvis, and St George Streets, on Davenport Hill, and in Rosedale were a prominent part of the scene and gave immediate evidence of the wealth that resided in Toronto, comfortable, verandahed, middle-class dwellings lining countless tree-shaded streets were much more typical of its domestic character in the first half of the century. Through the Depression and two world wars, Torontonians—or those, at least, who were not oppressed by poverty—took pleasure in a relatively secure existence, enjoying sports, imported theatre, an active musical life, their church, the annual Canadian National Exhibition (closed during the wars), and the pleasuregrounds of Sunnyside and the Island. They were indifferent to the resentments of other Canadians at Toronto's pervasive economic power; to the slings cast by non-Torontonians, particularly English visitors, at its dullness, its lack of style, its dead Sundays, its cultural mediocrity—though in 1913 Rupert Brooke saw nothing to take exception to, while finding little to single out for praise but the 'normal', 'healthy', 'cheerful' aspects of Toronto. He settled for an equivocal and probably deserved summation: 'It is all right.'

In the three decades after the Second World War the look and tone of the city have altered profoundly. For one thing, the composition of the population has changed, producing great ethnic diversity. In 1951 people of British origin accounted for 70 per cent of the population; in 1971, the year of the last census, they represented 45 per cent. In a population of over two million in Metropolitan

Toronto, there were more than a quarter of a million residents of Italian origin; people of Jewish, German, French, Asiatic, Ukrainian, and West Indian backgrounds accounted for other sizeable groups, who live (not always together) in both the city and the boroughs. In building lives for themselves here they have made Toronto more truly cosmopolitan, loosening it up, enlivening and otherwise improving run-down residential areas, using its green spaces, contributing an immense variety to the restaurants, foods, and products that were formerly so limited and unexceptionable.

In 1948 it became clear that Toronto and the growing municipalities that surrounded it required a single governmental structure. A two-tiered federation came into being in 1953: a metropolitan council, the central government, would share its powers with thirteen municipalities, which would be responsible for the administration of certain services. (In 1966 the municipalities were reduced to six boroughs: Toronto, East York, Etobicoke, York, North York, and Scarborough.) The needs of city government then outgrew the 1899 City Hall. A surprising spirit of civic enthusiasm and pride came to life in the events that surrounded the building of a new one: the unsatisfactory first plan (1955); the opposition of the electorate to a new building; agreement on procedure; an international competition, attracting 520 entries; the excitement caused by Viljo Revell's winning design; the opening of the new City Hall in 1965; a controversy over the purchase of Henry Moore's *The Archer*, chosen to grace the forecourt; and the violent and successful opposition to the proposed demolition of the Old City Hall. Revell's building, a majestic and imaginative sculptural creation, attracted world-wide attention and quickly implanted itself in the affections of the people, who use Nathan Phillips Square in winter and summer. It became the living centre of the city, as the architect and councillors and their advisors intended it should.

The new City Hall marked the beginning of a building boom. In 1971 more money was spent on construction in Toronto than in any other city in the world. Massive office complexes began to transform the old city skyline that had long been dominated by the Royal York Hotel and the Bank of Commerce, and bleak high-rise apartment developments spread into the outlying areas of Metro. Growth was self-generating, for the city was an attractive market for foreign investment and the financial capital of Canada, but it was unchecked, and people far removed from the power structure at City Hall—controlled by politicians and greatly influenced by developers—became alarmed.

Prior to this, from the late fifties on, certain inner-city neighbourhoods began to be renewed by middle-class people who had rejected suburban living and saw in the rundown Victorian houses standing on blighted streets potentially attractive places to live. These neighbourhoods were especially valued for combining elements of urban living that are almost mutually exclusive in other North American cities: single-family dwellings, shops, and entertainment. Creating new neighbourhoods out of old was linked with the felt need to preserve the city's contacts with its past. For, unlike Georgian Toronto, which has almost disappeared, some fine, vulnerable monuments of Victorian Toronto still existed and had a chance of surviving the inroads of development if enough interest was shown in them. Community organizations came into being that endeavoured to safeguard both these environments. And as lower-middle-class and working-class people began to feel their security threatened by development forces—particularly by the transformation of low-cost housing into expensively renovated 'town houses'—they too formed citizen-groups and took their concerns and protests to City Hall.

Such involvement made citizens realize that they could assist in shaping the city to their needs and led some people who had been relatively inactive politically to run for alderman. The council elected in 1972 was labelled 'reformist' and it became more so in 1974. Nonetheless, widely divergent points of view were revealed by the twenty-three councillors, who in 1975 could be characterized as 'old guard', moderates, 'soft line' reformers, and radicals—these last being aldermen who would remove the property industry entirely from City Hall politics and would have city government function in the interests of ordinary people. The moderate approach has so far carried the day, in true Toronto fashion. At this crucial stage in the city's development some of the issues that city planners are studying and that are discussed at length in council (with inevitable conflicts and crises) are housing policy and zoning density, decentralization of growth, slowing down office construction, providing more parkland, and protecting and enhancing neighbourhoods—all important factors in retaining and improving Toronto's present quality of life. But perhaps the best hope for its future prospects lies in the fact that these issues have engaged the attention of a very large number of people who have a passionate interest in the city's welfare and who watch the decisions of council closely.

Dull old Toronto is not so dull any more. To those mundane qualities of orderliness, safety, and cleanliness that were long valued above exciting, stylish amenities—and are now considered remarkable by outsiders—can be added sophisticated pleasures of big-city life: countless good restaurants, a stimulating mix of indigenous and imported cultural activities, new possibilities for leisure-time enjoyment, a more cosmopolitan flavour, and a great increase in the city's visual attractiveness (which these photographs by John de Visser show). But remnants of its conservative past still cling to Toronto, giving it individuality, ensuring that it will follow its own course (while allowing some play of reformist action)—even though to the casual viewer it might seem to have turned into a typical capitalist metropolis. Toronto has now become celebrated, to the surprise of Torontonians. They are little surprised, however, by the reason for this: Toronto's reputation as an exception to the trend that large North American cities are offering more dissatisfactions than pleasures to too many people. Toronto has always had its own ideas of what is good.

WILLIAM TOYE

2. UNION STATION, FRONT STREET WEST: GREAT HALL

NINETEENTH–CENTURY COMMERCIAL BUILDINGS ON FRONT STREET EAST

NINETEENTH–CENTURY COMMERCIAL BUILDINGS ON COLBORNE STREET

5. BANK OF MONTREAL, FRONT AND YONGE STREETS, FROM O'KEEFE CENTRE

BANK OF MONTREAL: DETAIL OF FRONTISPIECE

8. ST JAMES' CATHEDRAL FROM ST JAMES' PARK, KING STREET EAST

7 (*left*). ST JAMES' CATHEDRAL REFLECTED IN THE WINDOW OF KARELIA,
FRONT STREET EAST

9. ST LAWRENCE MARKET: CROSSING FRONT STREET FROM THE NORTH MARKET
   (WITH THE CUPOLA OF ST LAWRENCE HALL BEHIND) TO THE SOUTH MARKET

11. BASEMENT KITCHEN IN THE MACKENZIE HOUSE

12 (*right*). THE MACKENZIE HOUSE, BOND STREET

14. IN FRONT OF NATHAN PHILLIPS SQUARE

13 *(left)*. CITY HALL

16. NATHAN PHILLIPS SQUARE: THE POOL

15 (*left*). NATHAN PHILLIPS SQUARE: THE SKATING RINK
THE OLD CITY HALL AND SIMPSON'S TOWER ARE IN THE BACKGROUND

OSGOODE HALL, QUEEN STREET WEST

(*left*). OSGOODE HALL: COW GATE

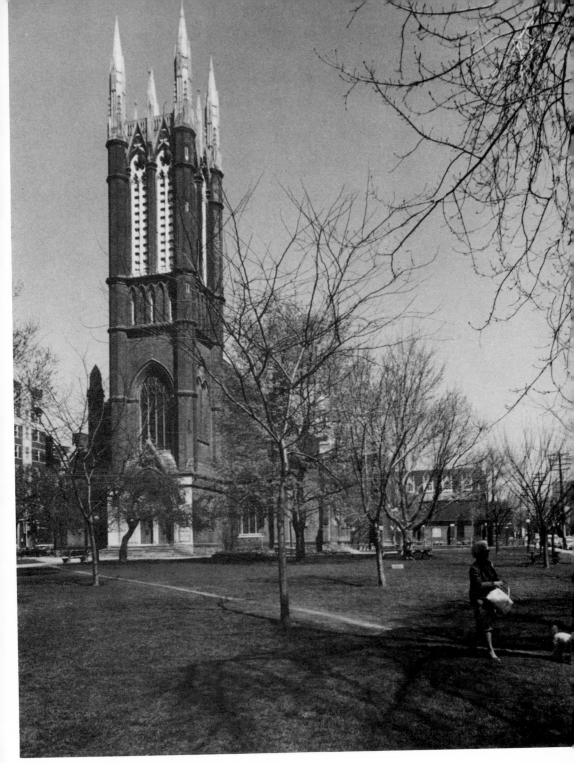

20. METROPOLITAN UNITED CHURCH, QUEEN AND BOND STREETS·

TORONTO-DOMINION CENTRE, WELLINGTON STREET WEST:
INSIDE THE OBSERVATION GALLERY

(left). FRUIT SELLER AT QUEEN AND YONGE STREETS

23. NOON-HOUR CONCERT IN COMMERCE COURT

THE OLD BANK OF COMMERCE BUILDING REFLECTED
IN A GLASS WALL OF COMMERCE COURT (WEST TOWER)

25. ROYAL ALEXANDRA THEATRE, KING STREET EAST

TORONTO SKYLINE FROM CENTRE ISLAND

Overleaf

(*left*). GOODERHAM BUILDING, WELLINGTON, CHURCH & FRONT STREETS

1 (*right*). ST JAMES' CATHEDRAL, KING STREET EAST, FROM THE ST LAWRENCE MALL

DETAIL OF THE MAIN DOOR OF OSGOODE HALL

(left). NATHAN PHILLIPS SQUARE: 'THE ARCHER' BY HENRY MOORE
WITH THE OLD CITY HALL AND SIMPSON'S TOWER IN THE BACKGROUND

. UNIVERSITY OF TORONTO CAMPUS, WITH THE SOLDIERS' TOWER IN THE BACKGROUND

(left).   HOUSE IN CABBAGETOWN

VIII.   AT YONGE AND EGLINTON IN WINTER

CAMPBELL HOUSE, QUEEN STREET AT UNIVERSITY AVENUE

CHINESE UNITED CHURCH
主日大崇拜：每禮拜晚七時半
請携友赴會
(一) 中英文兒童主日學：每禮拜日下午二時
(二) 英文補習班：續收新生
(三) 研經班：每禮拜日下午二時
(四) 婦女會（英文班／入籍班）每星期五下午二時半
(五) 青年（球賽活動／靈修研經班）每星期六晚八時
歡迎各界僑胞參加
李耀宸牧師電話：WA2-7444
EM4-7056

(*above*). THE HENRY MOORE
...PTURE CENTRE, ART GALLERY OF
...ARIO. DISPLAY OF ORIGINAL
...TERS. GIFT OF HENRY MOORE,
...3-4

(*right*). WOMAN, 1957/58, BY
...RY MOORE. ORIGINAL PLASTER IN
...HENRY MOORE SCULPTURE CENTRE,
...GALLERY OF ONTARIO. GIFT OF
...RY MOORE, 1973

(*left*). CHESTNUT STREET IN CHINATOWN

30. THE GRANGE, ART GALLERY OF ONTARIO: THE STAIRHALL

THE GRANGE, ART GALLERY OF ONTARIO

32. QUEEN'S PARK CRESCENT, WITH HYDRO PLACE IN THE BACKGROUND

33 (right). PARLIAMENT BUILDINGS: DETAIL OF STONE SCULPTURE

34, 35. PARLIAMENT BUILDINGS: DETAILS OF STONE SCULPTURE

36 (*right*). AERIAL VIEW OF THE PARLIAMENT BUILDINGS
AND THE UNIVERSITY OF TORONTO CAMPUS

37. CONVOCATION HALL, WITH UNIVERSITY COLLEGE IN THE BACKGROUND

38. UNIVERSITY COLLEGE TOWER, WITH THE CANADIAN VOLUNTEERS' MEMORIAL (1866)

59. UNIVERSITY COLLEGE: MAIN ENTRANCE

40. UNIVERSITY OF TORONTO: WAR MEMORIAL AND SOLDIERS' TOWER

41 (*right*). UNIVERSITY OF TORONTO: TRINITY COLLEGE CHAPEL, HOSKIN AVENUE

42. UNIVERSITY OF TORONTO: JOHN P. ROBARTS RESEARCH LIBRARY

3. KNOX COLLEGE, ST GEORGE STREET

5. ROYAL ONTARIO MUSEUM: MARBLE BAS-RELIEF PANEL, CHINESE, MING DYNASTY

4 (left). ROYAL ONTARIO MUSEUM: MARBLE MILITARY TOMB FIGURE,
CHINESE, MING DYNASTY

46. ROYAL ONTARIO MUSEUM: WROUGHT-IRON GATE,
NORTH ITALIAN, LATE SEVENTEENTH CENTURY

47, 48. YORKVILLE AVENUE

49. SHOP ON HAZELTON AVENUE (NORTH OF YORKVILLE)

50 (*right*). MARKHAM STREET

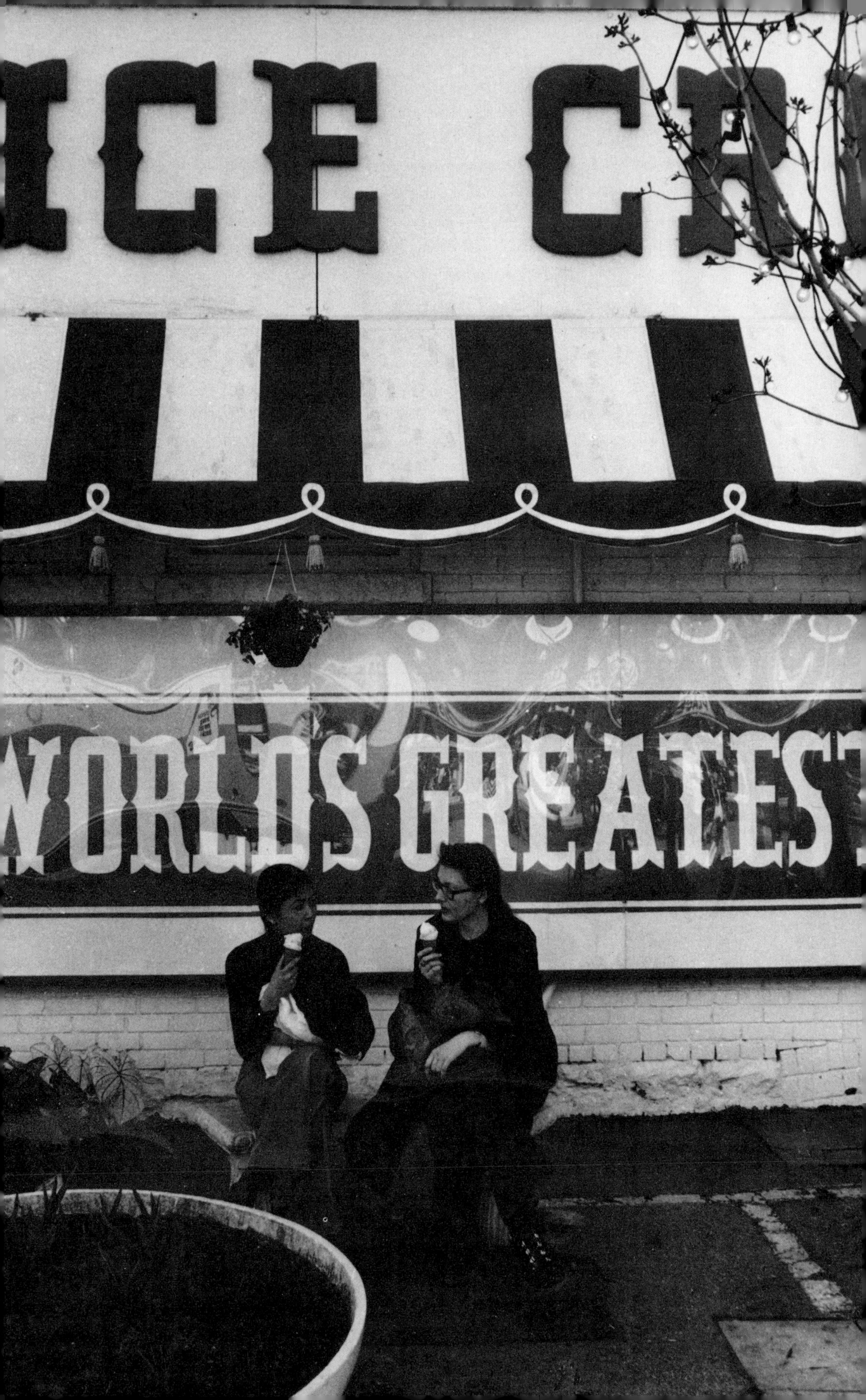
ICE
WORLDS GREATES

52. BLOOR STREET EAST, NEAR YONGE STREET

51 (*left*). BLOOR AND MARKHAM STREETS

54. BENEATH THE BLOOR VIADUCT

53 (left). HOUSES IN ROSEDALE

56. FRONT STREET EAST AT PARLIAMENT

55 (left). ST PAUL'S CHURCH, BLOOR STREET EAST

58. GOODERHAM AND WORTS DISTILLERIES, TRINITY & MILL STREETS

57 (*left*). A HOUSE IN CABBAGETOWN

. A PARTICIPANT IN 'CARAVAN', IN FRONT OF THE ENOCH TURNER SCHOOLHOUSE

(left). LITTLE TRINITY CHURCH, KING STREET EAST

61. ANTIQUE SHOP ON QUEEN STREET EAST

62 (*right*). 'PINECREST' ON PINE CRESCENT IN THE BEACHES

63. KEW BEACH

64, 65. KEW BEACH

7. SCARBOROUGH BLUFFS

5 (*left*).   SCARBOROUGH CIVIC CENTRE, MC COWAN AND ELLESMERE ROADS

8. UNIVERSITY OF TORONTO: SCARBOROUGH COLLEGE

30. ONTARIO SCIENCE CENTRE, DON MILLS ROAD: RECEPTION BUILDING

31. VICTORIAN RAILWAY STATION
IN TODMORDEN MILLS PARK

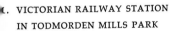

29 (*left*). METRO TORONTO ZOO,
MEADOWVALE ROAD, SCARBOROUGH

72. BROADWAY AND REDPATH AVENUES, NORTH TORONTO

73 (*right*). ALEXANDER MUIR PARK, YONGE STREET AND LAWRENCE AVENUE

75. HOGG'S HOLLOW PUBLIC GOLF COURSE

74 (*left*). GIBSON HOUSE, YONGE STREET, WILLOWDALE

76. LAND SAILING AT YORK UNIVERSITY

77 (right). SPECTATORS AT WOODBINE RACETRACK.
COPPER-TUBING SCULPTURE BY BILL KETTLEWELL

79. YORKDALE SHOPPING CENTRE, DUFFERIN STREET & HIGHWAY 401

78 (*left*). BLACK CREEK PIONEER VILLAGE, STEELES AVENUE AT JANE STREET

PLAZA OF THE TORONTO-DOMINION CENTRE

(left). CASA LOMA: THE STABLES

X. QUEEN'S PARK, WITH AN EQUESTRIAN STATUE OF EDWARD VII

XI (*right*). CHATSWORTH RAVINE IN WINTER

I. THE NATIONAL BALLET OF CANADA: 'SWAN LAKE'

XIV. SCARBOROUGH BLUFFS

THE TRAINING VESSEL 'PATHFINDER' AND SAILBOATS
IN LAKE ONTARIO, OFF GIBRALTAR POINT (THE ISLAND)

XVI. HOUSES OF THE 1880s ON ROBERT STREET

82, 83. KENSINGTON MARKET

KENSINGTON MARKET

86. HOUSE AND GARDEN ON BELLEVUE AVENUE

87. FIREHALL, COLLEGE STREET AND BELLEVUE AVENUE

SIAMO FATTE COSI
SEGUE
I GIORNI DELL IRA
ADULT ENTERTAINMENT

, 89, 90. THE ITALIAN DISTRICT, COLLEGE STREET WEST OF BATHURST

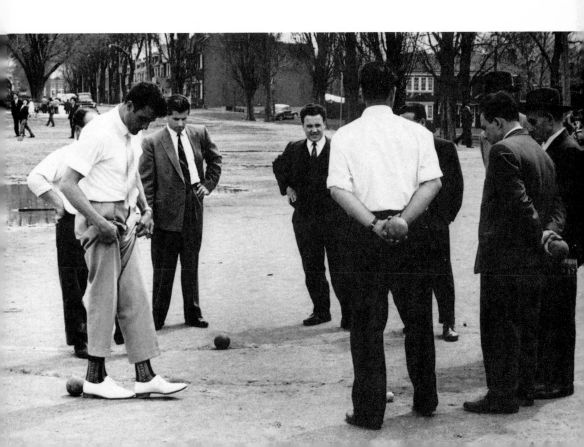

91. QUEEN STREET WEST

92. NIAGARA STREET

94. OLD FORT YORK, LAKESHORE BOULEVARD AND BATHURST STREET

93 (*left*). VICTORIA MEMORIAL PARK, WELLINGTON STREET WEST:
 WAR OF 1812 MONUMENT

5. THE MARINE MUSEUM IN THE EXHIBITION GROUNDS

6 (*left*). SUNNYSIDE BEACH

7. ROYAL HORSE SHOW: HACKNEY DRIVING CLASS

98. GRENADIER POND, HIGH PARK:
DUCKS BEING FED BY
THE TORONTO HUMANE SOCIETY

100 (*right*). DAM ON THE HUMBER RIVER

99 (*left*). NATURE WALK IN HIGH PARK

101. THE FORUM, ONTARIO PLACE: THE TORONTO SYMPHONY ORCHESTRA
(GUEST CONDUCTOR: ARTHUR FIEDLER)

102 (right). ONTARIO PLACE AND MARINA, WITH THE CN TOWER IN THE DISTANCE

103. FREIGHTER IN TORONTO HARBOUR

104 (*right*). PAINTING A FREIGHTER IN TORONTO HARBOUR

105. A FERRY HEADED FOR CENTRE ISLAND

106 (*right*). CENTRE ISLAND

8. CENTRE ISLAND IN WINTER,
WITH THE CHURCH OF
ST ANDREWS-BY-THE-LAKE
IN THE BACKGROUND

9 (*right*). CENTRE ISLAND,
SOUTH SHORE

07 (*left*). KIWANIS PICNIC,
CENTRE ISLAND

111. MARIPOSA FOLK FESTIVAL, CENTRE ISLAND

NOTES

Front cover; plates 9 and 10. The area of King, Jarvis, and Front Streets was designated for use as a market-place in 1803 and there has been a market there ever since. In 1831 a market building was erected on King Street that doubled as a market and town hall after 1834. It was left to its market use when the City Hall of 1844 was built (to the south, facing Front Street), but the market building burnt in the great fire of 1849. The following year ST LAWRENCE HALL was built on the same site—a handsome three-storey Neo-Classical building that housed shops, a market (entered from King Street, this was behind the Hall and backed on Front Street, as the North Market does today), and an attractive assembly room for concerts, lectures, balls, etc. The Hall saw twenty-five years of activity as a cultural centre until the Grand Opera House (1874) on Adelaide East and other theatres appeared in the growing city; it then declined physically and in every other way. Fortunately it was not removed, and in 1967 it was beautifuly restored. Its assembly room on the second floor is once more available for public use, and the rest of the building houses the offices and rehearsal halls of the National Ballet of Canada.

A new market building was part of the restoration. The Saturday morning ST LAWRENCE MARKET—which extends into a building south of Front Street that was erected around the 1844 City Hall—is not only the most venerable but perhaps the most beloved institution in the city.

1. AERIAL VIEW. Bottom to top: Union Station and the Royal York Hotel (1928), both facing Front Street, with the Royal Bank Plaza, under construction, to the right; the Toronto-Dominion Centre behind, of which the highest tower is 56 storeys; the First Bank Tower (Bank of Montreal) behind that, which will be 72 storeys when it is completed; the Simpson tower to the right; the Four Seasons Sheraton Hotel to the left and the City Hall behind, commanding Nathan Phillips Square on Queen Street West.

2. UNION STATION. Designed by John Lyle and built mainly in 1915-20, it was not opened until August 1927 because of a delay in the construction of a raised viaduct and trackage. A building that has strong associations for many, it is Toronto's most important monument to the early twentieth-century belief that the railroad station, as the symbol of modern progress, deserved the most imposing architectural form possible. Drawing on the grandeur and imperial associations of classical architecture, the Union Station (like many other North American stations) was modelled on the great baths of the Roman period. Its exterior colonnade and its immense ticket lobby or Great Hall, in pale pink and grey marble and with a vaulted ceiling 88 feet high, created an awe-inspiring environment for the traveller, to whom it was intended to represent the entrance to a great city. Even today, when its transportation role has altered, the Union Station is still an impressive 'open gate' to Toronto. It was threatened with demolition when development of the Front Street area (Metro Centre) was considered in the late sixties and early seventies, but it was saved—for the time being at least.

3, 4. NINETEENTH-CENTURY COMMERCIAL BUILDINGS. Those on Front Street East (1876), built as warehouses and wholesale establishments, were given stylized architectural forms to advertise the companies behind the façades and to ornament the city. The two blocks on Colborne Street were designed by E. J. Lennox and show the changes in architectural style at the end of the century, from the round-arched Romanesque detail of the building on the left (c.1885) to the quieter, more classical forms of the building on the right (c.1900).

5, 6. BANK OF MONTREAL (1885). Prominently situated in the angle of the intersection of Yonge and Front Streets, the main branch of the Bank of Montreal was one of Toronto's most imposing buildings in the nineteenth century. Indeed, for its monumental scale, its controlled use of flamboyantly romantic carved decorations—as in the frontispiece shown in plate 6—and its impressive banking hall, it remains an outstanding example of nineteenth-century business architecture. Its appearance today is slightly spoiled by the shape, colour, and letter-forms of its anachronistic signs.

7, 8, III. There was a small wooden church on the site of ST JAMES' CATHEDRAL in 1807. Enlarged in 1818-19, it was replaced by a stone church in 1833. It burned down in 1839 and was replaced in the same year by a church that was destroyed in the fire of 1849. The present Gothic Revival building (by Frederic William Cumberland) was begun in 1850, opened in 1853, and was finally completed in 1874, the year the spire was built. The grounds are a city park.

9, 10. ST LAWRENCE MARKET. See the first note (*Front cover*).

11,12. Originally part of a row of three houses, MACKENZIE HOUSE (c.1850) was presented to William Lyon Mackenzie (see the Introduction) by a committee of friends in 1859, nine years after he had returned to Toronto from exile in the United States. It is now owned by the city and run by the Toronto Historical Board as a museum.

13-16, IV. CITY HALL (1965). In this famous building, designed by the Finnish architect Viljo Revell (1910-64), the curved towers (27 and 20 storeys respectively) surround a domed council chamber, which rests on a podium. It stands on Nathan Phillips Square, named after the mayor whose enthusiasm contributed greatly to the project in its early days. See also the Introduction and the note on plate IV.

17-19, V. OSGOODE HALL houses the Supreme Court of Ontario and the Law Society of Upper Canada. The east wing was built in 1829-32 and named after William Osgoode, the first Chief Justice of Upper Canada. In 1844-6 the west wing was built and it was joined to the east wing, which was probably altered at this time, by an arcade surmounted by two storeys topped by a dome. This central portion was replaced in 1857-60 by a larger building bearing the façade we see today. The ornate iron fence containing six 'cow gates' (as protection against the cows from a neighbouring farm) was built in 1868. The streetcar in plate 17 is one of the Witt streetcars, familiar to Torontonians from 1921 until the opening of the Yonge Street subway in 1954, pressed into service as a sightseeing car.

20. METROPOLITAN UNITED CHURCH (1872). At the time it was built, this' was the world's largest Methodist church. The interior was destroyed by fire in 1928. (The text of the Sunday evening service on January 30 was '. . . the God that answereth by fire, let him be God' (1 Kings 18:24). Less than twelve hours later the church caught fire.) It was redesigned and rebuilt in 1929.

22, IX. TORONTO-DOMINION CENTRE (1967-74), designed by Mies van der Rohe, is composed of a single-level Banking Pavilion and three towers, the highest of which is the 56-storey Toronto Dominion Bank Tower, which houses the Observation Gallery.

23, 24. COMMERCE COURT (1972-4) was designed by I. Mario Pei as the head office of the Canadian Imperial Bank of Commerce. It preserves the old Canadian Bank of Commerce building (1929-31, Darling & Pearson)—at 34 storeys the tallest building in the British Empire for many years—as the focal point of an immense new development, which includes four towers (the tallest, the West Tower, is 57 storeys), an underground shopping mall, and a large open fountain court, which during the summer is a lunchtime attraction for office workers in the financial district.

25. ROYAL ALEXANDRA THEATRE (1907). In this elegant Edwardian theatre, designed by John Lyle, Torontonians have seen most of the famous names of the American and English stage. It would have been demolished in the sixties if Mr Ed Mirvish had not purchased it. After being beautifully restored, it reopened in 1963.

26. CAMPBELL HOUSE (1822). The elegant Georgian house of Chief Justice William Campbell (1758-1834) was originally built on Duke Street (Adelaide East) and had a view of the bay down Frederick Street. In the twentieth century it was used for business purposes until demolition was threatened. The Sir William Campbell Foundation, formed by the Advocates' Society, financed its move in 1972 to its present site, where it is being restored. Now used as a meeting-place for the Advocates' Society, it is open to the public. It is the third oldest residential building in Toronto, the other two being The Grange (plates 30 and 31) and the officers' quarters at Fort York (1816).

28, 29. The Henry Moore Collection in the ART GALLERY OF ONTARIO is the largest public collection of Moore's work in the world, virtually all of it a gift of the artist. It contains over four hundred pieces that include bronzes, original plaster sculptures, maquettes, as well as drawings, etchings, woodcuts, and lithographs. Selected pieces are displayed in the Henry Moore Sculpture Centre, a wing of the greatly enlarged Art Gallery of Ontario, which opened in 1974. The original buildings of the Art Gallery of Ontario were erected in 1918, 1926, and 1935, facing Dundas Street and adjoining The Grange (see the note following).

30, 31. THE GRANGE was built in 1817 by D'Arcy Boulton Jr, in the style of a Georgian manor house, outside of York on 100 acres that stretched from Queen Street north to Bloor. It remained in the Boulton family for nearly 100 years. In 1875 Mrs W.H. Boulton married Goldwin Smith, for whom changes were made and a library was added. She willed The Grange to the Art Museum of Toronto and it housed the Museum's collection from 1913 to 1918. It is part of the Art Gallery of Ontario and was restored in 1973 to represent a Gentleman's house of 1835.

32. The home of Ontario Hydro, HYDRO PLACE (1975), with its curved mirror sidewall (2,660 panels), does not have a heating plant. Three thermal reservoirs, comprising the world's largest energy conservation bank, store heat from solar radiation, artificial lighting, equipment, and people.

33-6. The provincial PARLIAMENT BUILDINGS opened in 1893. They were under construction at the same time as the Old City Hall and the ornament has the same densely patterned, almost Celtic quality that was the trade mark of the Romanesque Revival. Built from the same Credit River sandstone as the Old City Hall, they are a far less successful design (by the American architect R.A. Waite).

37. CONVOCATION HALL (1907), on the campus of the University of Toronto, was designed by Darling & Pearson and was modelled on the Sorbonne in Paris.

38, 39. Frederic William Cumberland's UNIVERSITY COLLEGE (1857-8)—with its picturesque tower, richly carved main entrance, mansard roofs, and Romanesque detailing—was considered 'the glory of the city' by Victorian Torontonians, who took pride in Anthony Trollope's comment that it was 'the only piece of collegiate architecture on the American continent worthy of standingroom in the streets of Oxford' (1862).

40. SOLDIERS' TOWER (1924). Dedicated to University of Toronto students who died in the First World War, this tower—modelled on Magdalen Tower in Oxford—stands next to Hart House, which accommodates athletic, social, and dining facilities for U of T students. A memorial screen dedicated to the dead of the Second World War connects the tower, by way of an arch, to University College.

41. TRINITY COLLEGE CHAPEL (1952). The pres-

ent Trinity College—a federated college of the University of Toronto, associated with the Anglican Church of Canada—was built in 1925 as a replica of the first (1851) on Queen Street West. The chapel was designed by Sir Giles Gilbert Scott, architect of Liverpool Cathedral —the most important Gothic Revival architect of the twentieth century.

42. The JOHN P. ROBARTS RESEARCH LIBRARY (1971-3) houses the Faculty of Library Science, the Thomas Fisher Rare Books Library, as well as the main research library of the University of Toronto. This monument of the 'new brutalism' is out of keeping with the scale of the campus, where it is known as 'Fort Book'.

43. KNOX COLLEGE (1915). This is the sixth training college in Toronto for ministers of the Presbyterian church; the first was founded in 1844 in a minister's house on James Street. The building is a classic example of 'scholastic Gothic' used for style and atmosphere.

44-6. While several galleries of the ROYAL ONTARIO MUSEUM were built from 1910 to 1913, the wing on Queen's Park Crescent was built in 1933. It originally incorporated five museums: the Royal Ontario Museums of Archaeology, Geology, Mineralogy, Palaeontology, and Zoology. Its collection of Chinese art and archaeology, much of it gathered in the 1920s and 1930s by George Crofts and William Charles White, Anglican Bishop of Honan, is one of the largest and most important of its kind.

47-9. The village of YORKVILLE, north of the First Concession (Bloor Street), was laid out in 1830 by Joseph Bloor, a brewer, and Sheriff William Botsford Jarvis. It was annexed to Toronto in 1883. Yorkville Avenue was well known in the middle 1960s for its coffeehouses and as a meeting-place for hippies. Since then much of it has been refurbished by a developer, Richard Wookey, and it is now a fashionable street of boutiques, art galleries, and craft shops etc.

50, 51. Mr Ed Mirvish, the proprietor of the discount store on Bloor Street West known as 'HONEST ED'S', bought up nineteenth-century houses on neighbouring Markham Street in the late fifties and sixties and created 'Mirvish Village', a community of antique shops and restaurants etc.

53. ROSEDALE, a residential district above Bloor Street east of Yonge, was lived in from the 1820s, when it was several miles north of York. It took its name from the house of Wil-

liam Botsford Jarvis, but it was not developed as a select neighbourhood of splendid houses, some of them with large grounds, until the 1880s.

55. ST PAUL'S CHURCH (1913). This monumental Anglican church, designed by E.J. Lennox in the style of a Gothic cathedral, is the third St Paul's. It stands next to the second (1860; enlarged in 1904), which is on the site of the first St Paul's (1842).

56. DALTON'S (1888). An example of grand architecture applied to an indispensable public utility. The building was originally part of the Consumers' Gas complex.

57, VI. CABBAGETOWN—between Sherbourne Street and the Don River, south of Carlton—was settled in the 1860s, 70s, and 80s by immigrant working-class people from Ireland and England who, contrary to normal Toronto custom, grew cabbages in their front yards. By the First World War the area had declined. It is now under great pressure for redevelopment and has become attractive to middle-class homeowners, who have renovated a great many of the old houses. The city is trying, by selective renewal, to preserve its heterogeneous character.

58. GOODERHAM & WORTS DISTILLERIES. William Gooderham and his brother-in-law James Worts founded their distillery in 1837. It grew to become one of the largest distilleries in the world and is now a complex of some forty well-designed buildings, erected periodically from 1859 into the present century. The buildings here were erected in the 1860s.

59. LITTLE TRINITY CHURCH was built in 1843 as an Anglican church for the people who worked at Gooderham and Worts (see note above). Designed by Henry Bower Lane in a rather severe, plain version of Perpendicular Gothic, it was intended to have a spire. It was restored after a fire in 1960.

60. The costumed girl was a contributor to the Dutch presentation for Caravan, an annual multicultural food and entertainment festival held in 'pavilions' all over the city and sponsored by non-commercial ethnic-cultural community organizations. The Dutch presentation was in the ENOCH TURNER SCHOOL-HOUSE (background), behind Little Trinity (above). It was built in 1848 by a brewer as a free school.

62. 'PINECREST'. The Beaches area developed in the late 1880s from a cottage colony on the shores of Lake Ontario. Even today, when the city has grown well past the Beaches, the district has retained much of the character of a heavily wooded small resort town. 'Pinecrest', built in the middle nineties, has more of the air of a country house, with its use of wraparound verandahs and wood siding, than is normal among the residences of Toronto.

66. SCARBOROUGH CIVIC CENTRE, designed by Raymond Moriyama to house the services of the municipal government of Scarborough, was opened by the Queen in 1973.

68. SCARBOROUGH COLLEGE (1966 & 1972) is a completely self-contained academic community twenty-one miles from the main campus of the University of Toronto. The strong forms of its concrete architecture complement its dramatic siting on the Scarborough escarpment.

69. METRO TORONTO ZOO, Phase One of which opened in August 1974, is a 710-acre zoological park in northeastern Metropolitan Toronto. Some 3500 animals (over 400 species), grouped in six zoo-geographical world regions, can be observed in settings that recreate their natural environments. It is one of the four largest public zoos in the world.

70. ONTARIO SCIENCE CENTRE (1969) is a complex of three interconnected buildings in an 18-acre park on the slopes of the Don Valley. They brilliantly display 550 interpretative exhibits of scientific principles and technological achievements, many of them participatory and audio-visual. The architect was Raymond Moriyama.

71. VICTORIAN RAILWAY STATION (1895). This station originally stood where King and Queen Streets East join, just west of the Don River. It is now on Pottery Road east of the Don Valley Parkway.

73. ALEXANDER MUIR PARK. Alexander Muir (1830-1906) was a school teacher who, in 1867, wrote the words and music of 'The Maple Leaf Forever', a popular patriotic song that was sung in schools until the Second World War when its pro-British imagery was seen to be invidious in the light of French-Canadian sensibilities.

74. GIBSON HOUSE (1851) was the spacious Georgian farm house of David Gibson (1804-64), the first city surveyor of Toronto and a follower of William Lyon Mackenzie in the Rebellion of 1837. It has ben restored and is open to the public.

77. WOODBINE RACE TRACK, which opened in

1956, is the largest track in North America (780 acres).

78. BLACK CREEK PIONEER VILLAGE was opened by the Metropolitan Conservation Authority in 1967. Five buildings on the Stong farm provided the nucleus and some twenty-five other buildings (the earliest, a barn, dates from 1809) were moved to the site and authentically restored. Other buildings are being added gradually.

80. CASA LOMA (1914). Recklessly and lavishly piling detail upon detail copied from European castles, Casa Loma is an architectural fantasy —both an incomparable folly and a rather endearing curiosity. It was designed by E.J. Lennox for Sir Henry Pellatt, who lived in it for only ten years. It reverted to the city for unpaid taxes in the 1930s and was eventually acquired by the Kiwanis Club of West Toronto. The palatial stables, built in 1906, are connected to the castle by an 800-foot tunnel.

81-5. The KENSINGTON MARKET area—which began on Kensington Avenue and spread into several neighbouring streets south of College and west of Spadina—was once predominately Jewish but is now about half Portuguese. For the shopper it is a lively and enticing neighbourhood for fruit and vegetables, meat and fish, dairy products, baked goods, and even clothing. Box-like apartment buildings have begun to replace the old houses, which were built as middle-class speculative dwellings in the 1880s.

87. COLLEGE STREET FIREHALL (c.1880; tower added in 1889). Built as a local landmark in a residential district that was considered important in the nineteenth century, this building was damaged by fire in 1972. It was rebuilt according to the original design.

93. VICTORIA MEMORIAL PARK. This monument —'to perpetuate the memory and deeds of the Officers, Non-Commissioned Officers and Men who gave their lives in the defence of Canada in the War of 1812-1815'—was erected in 1902.

94. British troops guarding Toronto were garrisoned at OLD FORT YORK, of which the officers' quarters (still standing) were built in 1816. Now surrounded by railway tracks and expressways, it was restored in the 1930s and is operated by the city as a museum.

96. The MARINE MUSEUM (1841)—formerly the Stanley Barracks, part of a military complex intended to replace Old Fort York—was opened as a museum in 1960. The *Ned Hanlan* —a maintenance tug and ice-breaker for the city from 1912 to 1965—was placed here in 1971. Ned Hanlan (1855-1908), the most celebrated Torontonian of his time, was a great oarsman who held the world's championship from 1880 to 1884.

97. The internationally famous ROYAL AGRICULTURAL WINTER FAIR and the ROYAL HORSE SHOW — commonly called 'the Royal' — in the Coliseum on the Canadian National Exhibition grounds, have been held annually every November since 1922, except for the war years.

98, 99. Part of what is now HIGH PARK in West Toronto was the property of John G. Howard (1803-90), the City Engineer and the architect of many Toronto buildings. He gave it to the city, who acquired it as a park in 1876, in return for a lifetime annuity for himself and his wife. His house, Colborne Lodge (1836), still stands and is open to the public.

101, 102. ONTARIO PLACE (1971). A Crown Corporation of the Government of Ontario, it is an innovative 96-acre leisure complex built on three man-made islands interlaced with lagoons and dominated by the dome of the 800-seat Cinesphere, containing a movie screen six storeys high.

At 1,815 feet, the CN TOWER, a telecommunications network, is the world's highest self-supporting structure. The tower, with its revolving restaurant, will open in 1976.

105-12. THE 'ISLAND' protecting Toronto's Inner Harbour—really several islands—is surely one of the most agreeable geographical features any city could be blessed with. It was once called the Peninsula and was joined to the eastern mainland by a sandbar that was washed away in 1858; the Gibraltar Point lighthouse (1806) at the western end of the Island is the oldest building in the City of Toronto. In the second half of the nineteenth century Centre Island, Hanlan's Point, and Ward's Island developed into highly popular pleasure-grounds, containing hotels, amusements, two yacht clubs, and many summer residences, from ornate frame mansions to modest cottages. In 1954 the islands were taken over by the Metropolitan Toronto Parks Commission and most of the 650 residences and all the hotels and amusement centres were demolished. (The small residential community remaining on Algonquin and Ward's Islands is one of the most distinctive and closely knit neighbourhoods in the city.) The 552 acres were turned into parkland with an amusement area for children on Centre Island. Stretching out in front of the striking Toronto skyline and only ten minutes away by ferry, the well-tended play-grounds, beaches, lagoons, and large areas of rural peacefulness (unspoiled by three private yacht clubs, a public marina, and the busy Island Airport) give to a million and a quarter summer visitors the refreshing illusion of re-moteness.

The annual Mariposa Folk Festival first took place in 1960 in Orillia, Ont. (the model for Stephen Leacock's Mariposa in *Sunshine Sketches of a Little Town*). Moved to Centre Island, it remains a highly popular weekend event every summer.

COLOUR PLATES

II. GOODERHAM BUILDING (1892). Sometimes called the 'Flat-iron' building because of its triangular shape, its corner tower was the symbol of the wealth and power of one of To-ronto's major commercial families.

III. ST JAMES' CATHEDRAL. See note on plates 7 and 8.

IV. OLD CITY HALL (1899). Before it was cleaned, the Old City Hall was seen as a dingy building whose soaring clock tower, facing Bay Street, meant Toronto to generations of citizens. The cleaning revealed the beautiful coloration of the red sandstone, quarried near the Credit River. The intricately carved detail-ing in the upper reaches of the building and the patterning in shades of pink and beige could be enjoyed for the first time in decades. All elements are combined in an organic whole that achieves the rich, picturesque effect the Canadian architect, E.J. Lennox, strove for in this impressive Romanesque Revival monu-ment—the high point in the Victorian archi-tecture of Toronto. The affection in which it has been held by Torontonians found expres-

sion in the public outcry that prevented its demolition in the 1960s.

Henry Moore's *Three-Way Piece No. 2*, known as *The Archer*, was purchased in 1969.

V. OSGOODE HALL. See note on plates 17-19.

VI. CABBAGETOWN. See note on plate 57.

VII. UNIVERSITY OF TORONTO CAMPUS. See note on plate 40.

IX. TORONTO-DOMINION CENTRE. See note on plate 22.

X. QUEEN'S PARK, behind the Parliament Build-ings, was opened in 1860 by the Prince of Wales, later Edward VII, the equestrian statue of whom once stood in Edward Park, Delhi, India.

XII. The CANADIAN NATIONAL EXHIBITION was originally called the Industrial Exhibition As-sociation of Toronto and was founded in 1879. It became the CNE (the 'Ex') in 1912—the largest annual exhibition in the world. The oldest building on the site was erected in 1905.

TORONTO

John de Visser

These views of Toronto, by one of the best known and most admired photographers in Canada, portray a city that has earned an international reputation as one of the most stimulating and agreeable cities in the modern world. With the eye of an artist and the skill of a craftsman, John de Visser has recorded its people, buildings old and new, streets and neighbourhoods, markets, monuments, cultural institutions, pastimes, parks, beaches, and even its weather, in images that include both the familiar and the surprising and are sometimes startlingly beautiful. It is a portrait that all Toronto-watchers — residents and visitors alike — will take great delight in.

The photographs are supplemented by a brief historical introduction and notes on the subjects by William Toye.

JOHN DE VISSER was born in Holland and came to Canada in 1952. He has been a full-time free-lance photographer since 1961, publishing in many North American magazines and contributing to more than fifty books. This is the sixth book to contain his photographs exclusively. Among the others are *Winter* (with Morley Callaghan), *This Rock Within the Sea* (with Farley Mowat), and *Heritage* (with Scott Symons).

WILLIAM TOYE, who has lived in Toronto all his life, is the author of *The St Lawrence*, editor of *A Book of Canada* and the *Supplement to The Oxford Companion to Canadian History and Literature*, and co-editor with Robert Weaver of *The Oxford Anthology of Canadian Literature*.

Cover design by FRED HUFFMAN. The cover subject is St Lawrence Hall (1850) on King Street East.

ISBN 19-540243-X

Oxford University Press